41 Insights From the Book of Revelation

Bisi Oladipupo

Springs of life publishing

41 INSIGHTS FROM THE BOOK OF REVELATION

Contents

To Jesus Christ, my Lord and Saviour—to Him alone that laid down His life that I might have life eternal. To Him that led captivity captive and gave gifts unto men (Ephesians 4:8). One of those gifts is writing!

Foreword

S everal years ago, the Book of Revelation was a mystery to me, and l hardly read it. To make matters worse, l noticed that the book was hardly referenced during sermons. However, when l started the reading, I found it difficult to comprehend.

Eventually, l continued to read it despite the difficulty, and as l did, light began to come. Now, l can truly say l enjoy the Book of Revelation.

Truth always unfolds, and there is still much more to be revealed in this book. However, the Book of Revelation is exactly what it says: "It is Revelation", i.e., an unfolding.

We know that *"All scripture is given by inspiration of God, and is profitable for doctrine, for reproof, for correction, for instruction in righteousness: That the man of God may be perfect, thoroughly furnished unto all good works"* (2 Timothy 3:16-17).

If we are to be thoroughly furnished unto all good works, we need to understand all scripture, including the Book of Revelation.

I do not claim to fully understand the Book of Revelation; far from it. Nevertheless, the Word of God is living, and each time l read it with the help of the Holy Spirit, l get more insight.

This book will give you some insights into the last book of the Bible—the Book of Revelation.

Enjoy the read!

Bisi

Introduction

The Book of Revelation is fascinating, and the first few chapters tell us about messages for the seven churches in Asia.

Each church had a different message which is still applicable today. As a result, it is clear that God's Word is living and for us today.

In each of these messages, there is so much profound truth, including rewards for His people and the personality of Jesus Christ.

Further in the book, we can see rewards, a description of the heavenly Jerusalem, the beast and his image, a warning about 666, the reality of heaven, hell, the thousand-year reign here on earth with our Lord Jesus Christ, the role of angels, and many other truths.

Let us have a closer look at this book.

Chapter One

The Lord Sees Everything Going On in Our Churches

E very church ordained by the Lord has an angel over it (Revelation 1:20), and from this scripture, it is clear our Lord Jesus Christ sees everything happening in our churches. As a matter of fact, the Bible clearly states that Jesus is in the midst of the candlesticks.

"And in the midst of the seven candlesticks one like unto the Son of man, clothed with a garment down to the foot, and girt about the paps with a golden girdle" (Revelation 1:13).

How differently we would conduct ourselves if we walked in this reality!

A message was sent to each of the churches in Asia (Revelation 1:4), and we have so much to learn from its content.

"*All scripture is profitable for doctrine, is profitable for doctrine, for reproof, for correction, for instruction in righteousness*" (2 Timothy 3:16). Therefore, all scripture includes the Book of Revelation.

Now, let's briefly look at some things our Lord Jesus Christ addressed.

Doctrine

Our Lord Jesus Christ addressed the issue of wrong doctrine. If wrong doctrine was addressed then, it is clear that it will be addressed today. This is why we must be students of the Word of God. We must ensure we rightly divide the Word of truth (2 Timothy 2:15). We must refuse to be blown away by "every wind of doctrine" (Ephesians 4:14). Note the word "wind". Wind comes and goes. Our hearts must be established in the Word of grace. We need to be like the Berean brethren who searched the scriptures daily to see whether those things were so (Acts 17:11).

So, what doctrine did our Lord address?

- The doctrine of Balaam (Revelation 2:14).
- The doctrine of Nicolaitans (Revelation 2:15).
- The doctrine of Jezebel, who taught and seduced the servants of the Lord to commit fornication and eat things sacrificed unto idols (Revelation 2:20-24).

We are told to speak things of sound doctrine (Titus 2:1).

What Jesus Commended

Works, labour, patience, standing against those that are evil, tribulation and poverty (but thou art rich), holding fast the name of the Lord in persecution, keeping the Word of His patience, and those who have not defiled their garments. Further account can be found in Revelation 2:2-3, 9-10, 13, 19; Revelation 3:1, 4, 8, and 10).

Other Things Jesus Warned the Churches About

You have left your first love, wrong teaching, having a name but dead, works not perfect before the Lord, and lukewarmness. Further account can be found in Revelation 2:20–23; Revelation 3:1–3, 16–18.

This is very sobering, but it's better we know the truth now and make the necessary adjustments. We must remember that the Lord rebukes and chastens those He loves. It is all for our good when we make the necessary adjustments and repent.

"Furthermore we have had fathers of our flesh which corrected us, and we gave them reverence: shall we not much rather be in subjection unto the Father of spirits, and live? 10 For they verily for a few days chastened us after their own pleasure; but he for our profit, that we might be partakers of his holiness. 11 Now no chastening for the present seemeth to be joyous, but grievous: nevertheless afterward it yieldeth the peaceable fruit of righteousness unto them which are exercised thereby" (Hebrews 12:9-11)

Chapter Two

An Insight Into the Roles of Angels

A ngels are mentioned throughout Scripture. We appear to see more angelic activity recorded in the Old Testament than in the New Testament. However, the word "angel" is found 72 times in the Book of Revelation. This shows the word is used more than in any other book of the Bible.

According to the Book of Hebrews, angels are ministering spirits:

"Are they not all ministering spirits, sent forth to minister for them who shall be heirs of salvation" (Hebrews 1:14).

Because angels are spirits, we cannot see them with our physical eyes except the Lord opens our eyes.

Now, let's briefly examine some angelic activities in the Book of Revelation.

Four angels were holding the four winds of the earth (Revelation 7:1).

If the Lord can use four angels to hold the four winds of the earth, what can our God not do?

Nobody can hold the wind, but God can.

God sent one angel to stand on each corner of the earth, not each corner of your town or village, but each corner of the earth. And only one angel is required to hold the wind.

The winds obey the Lord: "*But the men marvelled, saying, What manner of man is this, that even the winds and the sea obey him*" (Matthew 8:27).

We see a description of an angel in Revelation 10:1-6 "*clothed with a cloud, rainbow upon his head, his face like the sun, his feet as pillars of fire. His voice as when a lion roareth, when he cried seven thunders uttered their voice, the angel stood upon the sea and upon the earth*".

Revelation 18:1 describes an angel with great power and the earth (not just a location) was lightened with his glory.

Next time you quote the scripture, "The angel of the Lord encampeth round about them that fear him, and delivereth them" (Psalm 34:7), it should have a greater meaning.

Revelation 16:5 speaks about the angels of the waters; Revelation 14:18 speaks about an angel with power over fire.

The good news is that we all have angels assigned to us.

"And I John saw these things, and heard them. And when I had heard and seen, I fell down to worship before the feet of the angel which shewed me these things" [9] *Then saith he unto me, See thou do it not: for I am thy fellowservant, and of thy brethren the prophets, and of them which keep the sayings of this book: worship God"* (Revelation 22:8-9).

Chapter Three

Who Jesus Is?

R evelation 19:13 describes **Jesus as the Word**: "*And he was clothed with a vesture dipped in blood: and his name is called The Word of God*".

The Bible we have is not just ink and paper; it is a person.

When we meditate on the Word, we are meditating on Jesus Christ. Jesus is also called the bread of life (John 6:35). This is why we need to meditate on the Word of God, and this is how we will partake of His flesh. John 1:14 also confirms to us that Jesus is the Word of God.

Revelation 3:14 reads, "*And unto the angel of the church of the Laodiceans write; These things saith the Amen, **the faithful and true witness**, the **beginning of the creation of God**...*"

Here, we can see Jesus Christ as the faithful, the true witness, and the beginning of the creation of God. This is further confirmed in Colossians 1:16 and John 1:3.

We need to be faithful just as our Lord Jesus Christ was faithful. What does it mean to be faithful? Obeying the Father at all times and doing things His way—when it is convenient and not convenient—when we feel like it and when we don't feel like it. To remain faithful, we must have an eternal perspective about things.

The book also reveals Jesus Christ as the first begotten of the dead, the prince of the kings of the earth;

Revelation 1:5: *"And from Jesus Christ, who is the **faithful witness**, and **the first begotten of the dead**, and the **prince of the kings of the earth**. Unto him that loved us, and washed us from our sins in his own blood"*

If there is a first begotten, then there is a second, third, and so on. The Book of 1 Corinthians 15:52 speaks that we shall rise again.

Hence, we need to live in the reality of this truth.

The Book of Revelation also gives us various facets of our Lord Jesus Christ.

Lamb   (Revelation 6:1)

Lion of the tribe of Judah   (Revelation 5:5)

Alpha and Omega   (Revelation 1:8).

He that liveth and was dead and alive for evermore   (Revelation 1:18)

He that holds the seven stars in His right hand (Revelation 1:20)

He that walks in the midst of the seven golden candlesticks (Revelation 1:20)

The first and the last (Revelation 2:8)

He that has the sharp sword with two edges (Revelation 2:12)

He that has the seven spirits of God (Revelation 3:1)

He that is Holy, He that is true, He that hath the key

Of David, He that opens and no man shuts and shuts (Revelation 3:7)

And no man opens.

The Amen, the faithful and true witness, the beginning of

The creation of God (Revelation 3:14)

These are further revelations about the person of Jesus Christ that we need to meditate upon.

Chapter Four

Heaven and Hell Are Real Places!

The Book of Revelation reveals in a bit more detail heaven, hell and everlasting fire. Everlasting fire is a place no one needs to go to, as Jesus Christ had paid the price for us all so that no one has to go there.

Scripture clearly states that everlasting fire was not prepared for man but for the devil and his angels (Matthew 25:41).

Hell

So, let us see briefly what the Book of Revelation reveals about hell.

It is a bottomless pit (Revelation 9:1)

A great furnace (Revelation 9:2)

Everlasting punishment (Revelation 14:11)

Death and hell are cast into the lake of fire   (Revelation 20:15)

New Heaven

Now, let's look at the new heaven

The city is pure gold like unto pure glass (Revelation 21:18)

The foundations of the wall of the city are garnished with all manner of precious stones: (Revelation 21:19)

No more death, sorrow, crying, nor pain   (Revelation 21:4)

The twelve gates are made of twelve pearls (Revelation 21:21)

The Lord God and the Lamb are the temple of it (Revelation 21:22)

Only those written in the Lamb's book of life will enter (Revelation 21:27)

No more curse (Revelation 22:3)

No more night and they shall reign for ever and ever (Revelation 22:5)

These are just a few things revealed about heaven and hell. Nobody needs to go to hell. Scripture is very clear, "*Who will have all men to be saved and come unto the knowledge of the truth*" (1 Timothy 2:4).

If you don't know the Lord yet, today is the day of salvation. The price has already been paid. All you need to do is call upon the Lord and be saved.

"*That if thou shalt confess with thy mouth the Lord Jesus, and shalt believe in thine heart that God hath raised him from the dead, thou shalt be saved. For with the heart man believeth unto righteousness; and with the mouth confession is made unto salvation*" (Romans 10:9-10).

"*For whosoever shall call upon the name of the Lord shall be saved*" (Romans 10:13).

Chapter Five

There Is a Spiritual World

T he spiritual world is real. We ourselves are spirit beings who live in a body. The Bible clarifies that we have three parts: spirit, soul, and body (1 Thessalonians 5:23).

In the Book of Ephesians, we are also told that we wrestle not against flesh and blood (Ephesians 6:12).

The Book of Revelation gives us a bit more insight. Revelation 17:3-24 gives us more insight into the spiritual world and how it influences our physical world. Revelation 17:18 reads, *"And the woman which thou sawest is that great city, which reigneth over the kings of the earth..."*

This is one reason we need to pray for those in authority.

We also find this echoed in other parts of scripture, *"...according to the prince of the power of the air, the spirit that now worketh in the children of disobedience"* (Ephesians 2:2).

The prince of this world cometh and has nothing in me (John 14:30).

Thank God we have victory through our Lord Jesus Christ. When we give our lives to Jesus Christ, we are translated from the kingdom of darkness into the kingdom of His dear Son (Colossians 1:13).

Chapter Six

There Are Rewards in Heaven

S alvation is free; however, we will be rewarded for what we do for the Lord in this world. This is why it is essential to prioritise the things of the kingdom of God.

There is a reason the Bible says we should *"seek first the kingdom of God and His righteousness"* (Matthew 6:33). It is only what we do for the Lord that we can carry out with us.

Revelation 14:13: *"And I heard a voice from heaven saying unto me, Write, Blessed are the dead which die in the Lord from henceforth: Yea, saith the Spirit, that they may rest from their labours; and **their works do follow them***".

The Bible says we carry nothing into this world and shall carry nothing out of it (1 Timothy 6:7). Therefore, the only thing that will follow us is our work.

The Book of Revelation provides insights into what rewards look like in heaven.

Some chapters have the phrase, *"He who overcomes and states the reward".*

Let's have a look at some of these verses:

Revelation 2:7: *"He that hath an ear, let him hear what the Spirit saith unto the churches;* ***To him that overcometh will I give to eat of the tree of life, which is in the midst of the paradise of God".***

Revelation 3:21: *"To him that* ***overcometh will I grant to sit with me in my throne,*** *even as I also overcame, and am set down with my Father in his throne".*

We can see one reward in heaven that the apostles received. It really pays to serve the Lord!

Revelation 21:14: ***"And the wall of the city had twelve foundations, and in them the names of the twelve apostles of the Lamb".***

This is there and will be there for eternity because they followed the Lord. It is simply wonderful!

Here, we see another reward of the apostles of the Lamb:

"Ye are they which have continued with me in my temptations. [29] And I appoint unto you a kingdom, as my Father hath appointed unto me; [30] That ye may eat and drink at my table

in my kingdom, and sit on thrones judging the twelve tribes of Israel" (Luke 22:28-29).

This tells us that the Lord really loves us, and the Lord loves people. God our Father decided to name the foundation of the wall of the New Jerusalem after the names of the twelve apostles of the Lamb. Simply amazing!

Other scriptures in the Bible also tell us that we will be rewarded!

*"For the Son of man shall come in the glory of his Father with his angels; and **then he shall reward every man according to his works** "* (Matthew 16:27).

While we are down here in this present world, we need to live with this reality in view; for the things we see are temporal, and the things which are not seen are eternal (2 Corinthians 4:18).

We will be rewarded, and everyone will give an account of his life to the Lord as believers. Therefore, in this life, our Lord's passion should be our own passion.

"Jesus saith unto them, My meat is to do the will of him that sent me, and to finish his work" (John 4:34).

The Lord told the crowds when they were looking for Him that it was because of the multiplication of bread and food they ate (John 6:26). He told them to labour not for that meat but for meat that has an everlasting reward.

"Labour not for the meat which perisheth, but for that meat which endureth unto everlasting life, which the Son of man

shall give unto you: for him hath God the Father sealed" (John 6:27).

At the end of it all, only our works will follow us (Revelation 14:13).

"Salvation is free but rewards are not free. You are rewarded for what you do".

Looking at the rewards laid up for the saints, whatever we go through on this side of eternity is "light affliction" compared to the glory that shall be revealed.

"For our light affliction, which is but for a moment, worketh for us a far more exceeding and eternal weight of glory" (2 Corinthians 4:17).

Chapter Seven

The Beast, His Image, and His Mark

There are severe warnings about worshipping the beast and his image and receiving his mark (Revelation 14:9-11).

Knowing the nature of God that is love (1 John 4:8), the Lord is warning His people. There would be no warnings if people had no choice about the matter. The mere fact that the Bible warns us against it shows that people will be able to resist it.

Scripture makes it clear that there would be those who resist worshipping the beast's image and getting his mark.

"And I saw thrones, and they sat upon them, and judgment was given unto them: and I saw the souls of them that were beheaded for the witness of Jesus, and for the word of God,

and which had not worshipped the beast, neither his image, neither had received his mark upon their foreheads, or in their hands; and they lived and reigned with Christ a thousand years" (Revelation 20:4).

The Bible speaks about the manner of the mark in Revelation 13:16-18.

Many have asked whether saints will be around during the time of the beast. The honest answer is it is not very clear; however, we can see the scripture in Revelation 20 that some people will have to resist the mark. It is also likely there will be some who will suddenly realise that Scripture is true and will resist the mark. Once again, the Lord will not warn us about the image and the mark if it cannot be resisted.

"*2 And I saw as it were a sea of glass mingled with fire: and them that had gotten the victory over the beast, and over his image, and over his mark, and over the number of his name, stand on the sea of glass, having the harps of God.* 3 And they sing the song of Moses the servant of God, and the song of the Lamb, saying, Great and marvellous are thy works, Lord God Almighty; just and true are thy ways, thou King of saints" (Revelation 15:2-3).

It will not be an easy time on earth.

Chapter Eight

Every Man Will Be Judged

W hatever we do is so important; if it were unimportant, there would be no judgement seat.

According to Scripture, we shall all be judged for what we have done in our bodies while here on earth.

"*And I saw a great white throne, and him that sat on it, from whose face the earth and the heaven fled away; and there was found no place for them. And I saw the dead, small and great, stand before God; and the books were opened: and **another book was opened, which is the book of life: and the dead were judged out of those things which were written in the books, according to their works***" (Revelation 20:11-12).

Some have said only those who don't know the Lord will be at the white throne judgement, but this is not what Scripture teaches.

21

The book of life would not be opened at the white throne if it were not necessary.

Scripture is clear that men will be judged according to what is written in the books.

This shows that what we do is important.

We are all important to God, and nothing we do is insignificant.

Every man will be judged.

*"For we must all appear before the judgment seat of Christ; that every one may receive the things done in his body, according to that he hath done, **whether it be good or bad**"* (2 Corinthians 5:10).

Note the above phrase highlighted, "***whether it be good or bad***".

"But why dost thou judge thy brother? or why dost thou set at nought thy brother? for we shall all stand before the judgment seat of Christ" (Romans 14:10).

Chapter Nine

The Scriptures Applies to Whosoever Will Believe

Nobody's names are written in the Bible; no special titles but "whosoever" will believe.

Heaven does not have designated rewards for special people but to "whosoever" will hear.

"He that hath an ear, let him hear what the Spirit saith unto the churches; To him that overcometh will I give to eat of the tree of life, which is in the midst of the paradise of God" (Revelation 2:7).

*"And the Spirit and the bride say, Come. And let him that heareth say, Come. And let him that is athirst come. **And whosoever will**, let him take the water of life freely"* (Revelation 22:17).

This is an open invitation for all.

Chapter Ten

God's Throne Is Described

"A *And immediately I was in the spirit: and, behold, a throne was set in heaven, and one sat on the throne. And he that sat was to look upon like a jasper and a sardine stone: and there was a rainbow round about the throne, in sight like unto an emerald. And round about the throne were four and twenty seats: and upon the seats I saw four and twenty elders sitting, clothed in white raiment; and they had on their heads crowns of gold. And out of the throne proceeded lightnings and thunderings and voices: and there were seven lamps of fire burning before the throne, which are the seven Spirits of God. **And before the throne there was a sea of glass like unto crystal: and in the midst of the throne, and round about the throne, were four beasts full of eyes before and behind** "*(Revelation 4:2-6).

What is happening around the throne is described (Revelation 5:11-14; Revelation 7:11-12).

Did you know that when we pray, we are actually approaching God's throne in Jesus' name?

*"For we have not an high priest which cannot be touched with the feeling of our infirmities; but was in all points tempted like as we are, yet without sin. **Let us therefore come boldly unto the throne of grace**, that we may obtain mercy, and find grace to help in time of need"* (Hebrews 4:15-16).

Jesus is seated down on the right hand of God's throne

*"Now of the things which we have spoken this is the sum: We have such an high priest, **who is set on the right hand of the throne of the Majesty in the heavens**"* (Hebrews 8:1).

*"Looking unto Jesus the author and finisher of our faith; who for the joy that was set before him endured the cross, despising the shame, and is **set down at the right hand of the throne of God**"* (Hebrews 12:2).

Chapter Eleven

Our Prayers Are Powerful

The Book of Revelation gives us an insight into what happens to our prayers. We live in this world by faith.

Don't ever think your prayers are not effective because they are.

"*And when he had taken the book, the four beasts and four and twenty elders fell down before the Lamb, having every one of them harps, and **golden vials full of odours, which are the prayers of saints**"* (Revelation 5:8).

"*And another angel came and stood at the altar, having a golden censer; and there was given unto him much incense, **that he should offer it with the prayers of all saints upon the golden altar which was before the throne.** And the smoke of the incense, **which came with the prayers of the saints, ascended up before God** out of the angel's hand*" (Revelation 8:3-4).

According to Scripture, we are saints if Jesus Christ is our Lord and Saviour.

"*To all that be in Rome, beloved of God, **called to be saints:** Grace to you and peace from God our Father, and the Lord Jesus Christ*" (Romans 1:7).

"*Unto the church of God which is at Corinth, to them that are sanctified in Christ Jesus, **called to be saints, with all that in every place call upon the name of Jesus Christ our Lord, both their's and our's**:*" (1 Corinthians 1:2).

Next time you pray, just picture your prayer ascending to God upon the golden altar before His throne (Revelation 8:4).

This should also give us confidence in our own prayers. There is only one throne where all the prayers go.

Our prayers are important.

Chapter Twelve

The Power of Associations

The Bible confirms that our associations are significant. Sometimes, we are told not to even invite certain people into our home.

"*10 If there come any unto you, and bring not this doctrine, receive him not into your house, neither bid him God speed: 11 For he that biddeth him God speed is partaker of his evil deeds*" (2 John 1:10-11).

"*10 If anyone comes to you and does not bring this teaching [but diminishes or adds to the doctrine of Christ], do not receive or welcome him into your house, and do not give him a greeting or any encouragement; 11 for the one who gives him a greeting [who encourages him or wishes him success, unwittingly] participates in his evil deeds*" (2 John 1:10-11; AMP).

We can see a similar concept in the Book of Revelation.

"*4 And I heard another voice from heaven, saying, **Come out of her, my people, that ye be not partakers of her sins**, and that ye receive not of her plagues*" (Revelation 18:4).

In the Book of Timothy (1 Timothy 5:22), we are warned not to be a partaker of another man's sin. From the scripture we have looked at in the Book of Revelation above, we can see that one way of partaking of another man's sin is by association.

This is further evidence that associations are crucial.

Further implications about associations can also be found in other places in Scripture:

"*14 Be ye not unequally yoked together with unbelievers: for what fellowship hath righteousness with unrighteousness? and what communion hath light with darkness? 15 And what concord hath Christ with Belial? or what part hath he that believeth with an infidel? 16 And what agreement hath the temple of God with idols? for ye are the temple of the living God; as God hath said, I will dwell in them, and walk in them; and I will be their God, and they shall be my people. 17 **Wherefore come out from among them, and be ye separate, saith the Lord, and touch not the unclean thing;** and I will receive you. 18 And will be a Father unto you, and ye shall be my sons and daughters, saith the Lord Almighty*" (2 Corinthians 6:14-18).

Has the Lord been warning you to stop associating with a certain person or group? There could be a very serious why.

Chapter Thirteen

There Are Books in Heaven

While this is implied in another chapter, it is good for us to see this separately.

What are books used for?

Books are used to record information. The Book of Revelation mentions various types of books: (Revelation 5:1; Revelation 10:9; Revelation 13:8; Revelation 20:12).

However, it is interesting that there is only one book of life (Revelation 13:8). According to Scripture, we know the Lord wants all men to be saved (1 Timothy 2:4), so this could be why there is no other book pertaining to the eternal place a person will spend eternity?

Do you know Jesus Christ as Lord and Saviour?

The Bible says people will be judged from the books (Revelation 20:12), which means things are being recorded daily while we are here on earth.

The remedy is simple. Walk as close as you know how with the Lord and judge yourself quickly. We also need to ask the Lord to forgive us when we do wrong (1 John 1:9).

We also need to receive the love of God. God is love (1 John 4:7), and He loves us.

Chapter Fourteen

Everything About God Is Holy

Our God is a holy God (1 Peter 1:16), and holiness is always associated with Him.

Did you even notice that we are referred to as "holy brethren" (Hebrews 3:1). We are also called to be holy (1 Peter 1:16; Ephesians 1:4).

So, what does 'holy' mean? In my own words, l would say, 'set apart, no faults, perfect, clear', and the list goes on. So, I looked up the word "holy" in a dictionary** and this is what it partly said, "Holy signifies perfectly pure, immaculate and complete in moral character" from King James Dictionary Online Edition.

As we look at the Book of Revelation, let us look at the word "holy".

The Lord is holy (Revelation 3:7; Revelation 4:8; Revelation 6:10).

The city is holy (Revelation 11:2; Revelation 21:2).

The angels are holy (Revelation 14:10).

The Apostles are holy (Revelation 18:10).

We are holy (Revelation 20:6).

The prophets are holy (Revelation 22:6).

Everything about our Lord is holy. Therefore, with this perspective, we must treat other people right, as this is part of being holy.

"Follow peace with all men, and **holiness**, without which no man shall see the Lord:" (Hebrews 12:14).

We perfect holiness by the fear of the Lord.

"Having therefore these promises, dearly beloved, let us cleanse ourselves from all filthiness of the flesh and spirit, perfecting holiness in the fear of God" (2 Corinthians 7:1).

Chapter Fifteen

Supernatural Light/The Holy Jerusalem

T he Book of Revelation gives us some detail about the New Jerusalem. Notice the word "New".

"And I saw a new heaven and a new earth: for the first heaven and the first earth were passed away; and there was no more sea. ² And I John saw the holy city, new Jerusalem, coming down from God out of heaven, prepared as a bride adorned for her husband. ²² And I saw no temple therein: for the Lord God Almighty and the Lamb are the temple of it. ²³ And the city had no need of the sun, neither of the moon, to shine in it: for the glory of God did lighten it, and the Lamb is the light thereof" (Revelation 21:1-2, 22-23).

This description is beyond human words. The Bible says the city does not need the sun or the moon to shine in it, for the glory of God lights it, and the Lamb is the light of it.

This is what we can call "Supernatural light".

"22 I saw no temple in the city, for the Lord God Almighty and the Lamb are its temple. 23 And the city has no need of sun or moon, for the glory of God illuminates the city, and the Lamb is its light" (Revelation 21:22-23).

Chapter Sixteen

Warning About Lukewarmness

While we have mentioned this briefly in a previous chapter, it will be good to look at it in a bit more detail.

Let us first look at the scripture the Lord spoke about lukewarmness in its proper setting.

"*14 And unto the angel of the church of the Laodiceans write; These things saith the Amen, the faithful and true witness, the beginning of the creation of God; 15 I know thy works, that thou art neither cold nor hot: I would thou wert cold or hot. 16 So then because thou art lukewarm, and neither cold nor hot, I will spue thee out of my mouth. 17 Because thou sayest, I am rich, and increased with goods, and have need of nothing; and knowest not that thou art wretched, and miserable, and poor, and blind, and naked: 18 I counsel thee to buy of me gold tried in the fire, that thou mayest be rich; and white raiment, that thou mayest be clothed, and that the shame of thy nakedness do not appear; and anoint thine eyes with eyesalve, that thou mayest see. [19] As many as I love, I rebuke and chasten: be zealous therefore, and repent"* (Revelation 3:14-19).

If you look at verse seventeen, this church did not know they were lukewarm. They said they had natural things but did not know their true spiritual condition (Revelation 3:17).

So, what was the remedy?

They were told to buy the Lord's gold tried in the fire, which would result in true riches. True gold here is the Word of God (Psalms 12:6).

And white raiment that they may be clothed. White raiment is the righteousness of the saints (Revelation 19:8).

And to remove obstacles that will hinder revelational knowledge. Eyes that they may see (Ephesians 1:18).

In summary, to keep hot, we must keep ourselves in the Word of God, walk in His righteousness, both positional and relational, and walk in revelational knowledge.

Chapter Seventeen

There Is a Place for Labour

Nobody likes the word 'labour', but this is necessary in the kingdom. It is only down here in this present world we get to labour and get our reward from the Lord.

"*And I heard a voice from heaven saying unto me, Write, Blessed are the dead which die in the Lord from henceforth: Yea, saith the Spirit, **that they may rest from their labours; and their works do follow them***" (Revelation 14:13).

Labour is work, and if we are to enter the various ministries and giftings while deploying and developing the talents the Lord has given us, it will involve labour.

"**12** *Salute Tryphena and Tryphosa, who labour in the Lord. Salute the beloved Persis, which laboured much in the Lord*" (Romans 16:12).

"*Now he that planteth and he that watereth are one: and every man shall receive his own reward according to his own labour*" (1 Corinthians 3:8).

God's grace enables us to labour in His vineyard; we just have to yield and grow in His grace.

This is Paul speaking here:

"*Whereunto I also labour, striving according to his working, which worketh in me mightily*" (Colossians 1:29).

Chapter Eighteen

The Gift of Repentance

In a previous chapter, we have looked briefly at what the Lord warned about in the churches. However, if you take time to look at the scriptures, the remedy was always repentance.

*"Remember therefore from whence thou art fallen, and repent, and do the first works; or else I will come unto thee quickly, and will remove thy candlestick out of his place, **except thou repent**"* (Revelation 2:5).

*"And **I gave her space to repent** of her fornication; and **she repented not**"* (Revelation 2: 21).

"As many as I love, I rebuke and chasten: be zealous therefore, and repent. 20 Behold, I stand at the door, and knock: if any man hear my voice, and open the door, I will come in to him, and will sup with him, and he with me" (Revelation 3:19-20).

The Lord corrects us because He loves us, and the wise receive correction from the Lord and repent. Repentance helps us get back on track.

Chapter Nineteen

The Glorified Bride

We are now the Bride of Christ. The parable of the ten virgins refers to us as the Bride of Christ (Matthew 25:1-13).

The Book of Revelation describes the glorified Bride of Christ. What an awesome experience that will be!

"*9 And there came unto me one of the seven angels which had the seven vials full of the seven last plagues, and talked with me, saying, **Come hither, I will shew thee the bride, the Lamb's wife.** 10 And he carried me away in the spirit to a great and high mountain, and shewed me that great city, the holy Jerusalem, descending out of heaven from God*" (Revelation 21:9-10).

Have you ever been invited to attend a marriage meal recently? Can you imagine what the marriage supper of the Lamb will be like?

"And he saith unto me, Write, Blessed are they which are called unto the marriage supper of the Lamb. And he saith unto me, These are the true sayings of God" (Revelation 19:9).

Chapter Twenty

We Are Kings and Priests

D id you know we are kings? We have been made kings and priests unto God through the sacrifice of Jesus Christ.

"*5 And from Jesus Christ, who is the faithful witness, and the first begotten of the dead, and the prince of the kings of the earth. Unto him that loved us, and washed us from our sins in his own blood, 6 And hath made us kings and priests unto God and his Father; to him be glory and dominion for ever and ever. Amen*" (Revelation 1:5-6).

A king in the natural has authority, and so do we spiritually. We need to meditate on who we really are in Christ, "kings and priests".

1 Peter 2: 9 says we are a royal priesthood, and Paul addressed the Corinthian church that they had reigned as "kings" (1 Corinthians 4:8).

John describes the New Jerusalem in the Book of Revelation and speaks about those who will bring their glory and honour into it.

"*24 And the nations of them which are saved shall walk in the light of it:* **and the kings of the earth do bring their glory and honour into it**. *25 And the gates of it shall not be shut at all by day: for there shall be no night there. 26 And they shall bring the glory and honour of the nations into it*" (Revelation 21:24-26).

 We believers of Christ are the kings of the earth.

Chapter Twenty-one

The Appearance of Jesus Revealed

T he Book of Revelation gives a description of our Lord Jesus Christ. You can ignore those paintings you see and look into Scripture for what Jesus Christ looks like. I know He can appear in various forms (Mark 16:12); however, let us look at the description the Book of Revelation gave us.

"*13 And in the midst of the seven candlesticks one like unto the Son of man, clothed with a garment down to the foot, and girt about the paps with a golden girdle. 14 His head and his hairs were white like wool, as white as snow; and his eyes were as a flame of fire; 15 And his feet like unto fine brass, as if they burned in a furnace; and his voice as the sound of many waters. 16 And he had in his right hand seven stars: and out of his mouth went a sharp twoedged sword: and his countenance was as the sun shineth in his strength*" (Revelation 1:13-16).

Let us look at this description briefly:

Head and hair: white like wool and white as snow

Eyes: flame of fire

Feet: fine brass as if they burned in a furnace

Voice: The sound of many waters

Countenance: As the sun shineth in his strength

We can all identify with the sun. The sun reflects in various degrees; here, the Bible says that Jesus Christ's countenance is like the sun shining in its full strength!

"*And his face was like the sun in all **its brilliance***" (Revelation 1:16; NLT).

"*His face [reflecting His majesty and the ⁽⁾Shekinah glory] was like the sun shining in [all] its power [at midday]*" (Revelation 1:16; AMP).

Meditate on that. What a glorious Lord we serve!

Chapter Twenty-two

Jesus Is the Amen

A men is a word that nearly everybody knows. It is the word that is said after prayer and means, "So be it".

However, did you know Jesus Christ is our "Amen"?

Jesus Christ, our Lord, has paid the ultimate price for us all, and it is because of Jesus Christ we can come unto God the Father. And when we ask anything according to His will in the name of Jesus Christ, the Father hears us (John 14:13).

"And unto the angel of the church of the Laodiceans write; These things saith the Amen, the faithful and true witness, the beginning of the creation of God" (Revelation 3:14).

From the above scripture, we can see that Jesus is the "Amen".

Jesus Christ is the "Amen"; the reason we get our prayers answered is all because of Jesus Christ.

"For all the promises of God in him are yea, and in him Amen, unto the glory of God by us" (2 Corinthians 1:20).

Chapter Twenty-three

Delivered From the Wrath to Come

S cripture clearly shows that believers have been delivered from the wrath to come (1 Thessalonians 1:10).

It is safe to say that before God's wrath, the saints still in this world would have been raptured.

In other scriptures, we are warned not to be partakers of the things that will result in the wrath of God; therefore, we are not appointed to wrath.

"*5 For this ye know, that no whoremonger, nor unclean person, nor covetous man, who is an idolater, hath any inheritance in* *the kingdom of Christ and of God. ⁶ Let no man deceive you with vain words: **for because of these things cometh the wrath of God upon the children of disobedience. ⁷ Be not** ye therefore partakers with them*" (Ephesians 5:5-7).

From the above scripture, we can see that God's wrath is not for saints.

"*For God hath not appointed us to wrath, but to obtain salvation by our Lord Jesus Christ*" (1 Thessalonians 5:9).

As we know that the Lord wants all men to be saved and come unto the knowledge of the truth (1 Timothy 2:4), anyone who calls upon the Lord Jesus Christ and accepts His sacrifice shall be saved. The Lord does not want anyone to perish.

Jesus Christ came so that we may obtain salvation. Do you know the Lord Jesus Christ?

So, when we see the wrath of God in the Book of Revelation (Revelation 6:17; Revelation 11:18), there is nothing to be concerned about as a believer in Jesus Christ.

Chapter Twenty-four

The Clouds Speak to Us!

I t is amazing that God can speak to us through creation.

Anytime you look up at the clouds, and while they may determine whether or not it will rain, there is something else very significant that the clouds are saying. They are saying, one day, Jesus Christ is coming!

*"**Behold, he cometh with clouds**; and every eye shall see him, and they also which pierced him: and all kindreds of the earth shall wail because of him. Even so, Amen"* (Revelation 1:7).

We can see from this scripture that Jesus Christ will come back with clouds.

"*Jesus saith unto him, Thou hast said: nevertheless I say unto you, Hereafter shall ye see the Son of man sitting on the right hand of power, and* **coming in the clouds of heaven**" (Matthew 26:64).

Chapter Twenty-five

Hidden Manna

T he Bible talks about "Hidden Manna" to those who overcome.

*"He that hath an ear, let him hear what the Spirit saith unto the churches; To him that overcometh **will I give to eat of the hidden manna**, and will give him a white stone, and in the stone a new name written, which no man knoweth saving he that receiveth it"* (Revelation 2:17).

This is some sort of supernatural food, as we know that the children of Israel were given manna to eat in the wilderness and referred to as "Angel's food" (Psalm 78:24-25). However, the manna in the Book of Revelation is called "Hidden Manna".

Chapter Twenty-six

White Stone

We are also told that those who overcome, according to Revelation 2:17, will also be given a white stone. But there is something special about this stone. Let us look again at the scripture:

*"He that hath an ear, let him hear what the Spirit saith unto the churches; To him that overcometh will I give to eat of the hidden manna, **and will give him a white stone, and in the stone a new name written, which no man knoweth saving he that receiveth it**"* (Revelation 2:17).

Again, this is supernatural as in the natural, the name would have to be written "on the stone" for it to be seen. So, this scripture is telling us that there will be a new name "in the stone". Just try to imagine that!

Heaven is a supernatural place so amazing beyond human reasoning to comprehend its beauty and awesomeness.

Chapter Twenty-seven

The Rainbow Speaks to Us!

In the scripture mentioned under the chapter "God's Throne is Described", we found out that there is a rainbow round about the throne. Let us look at this briefly.

*"2 And immediately I was in the spirit: and, behold, a throne was set in heaven, and one sat on the throne. 3 And he that sat was to look upon like a jasper and a sardine stone: and **there was a rainbow round about the throne, in sight like unto an emerald**"* (Revelation 4:2-3).

In the Book of Genesis, the Lord made a covenant with every living creature just after the flood that He would not destroy the world with water again.

*"13 **I do set my bow in the cloud,** and it shall be for a token of a covenant between me and the earth. 14 And it shall come to pass, when I bring a cloud over the earth, that the bow shall be seen in the cloud: 15 And I will remember my covenant, which is between me and you and every living creature of all flesh; and the waters shall no more become a flood to destroy all flesh"* (Genesis 9:13-15).

The rainbow in the cloud signifies that God will not destroy the world with water again. We are also told that a rainbow is round about the throne of God.

So, next time you see a rainbow, be reminded of the throne of God!

Chapter Twenty-eight

Songs Are Being Sung in Heaven

A s we speak now, songs are being sung in heaven.

"*8 And the four beasts had each of them six wings about him; and they were full of eyes within: and they rest not day and night, saying, Holy, holy, holy, Lord God Almighty, which was, and is, and is to come. 9 And when those beasts give glory and honour and thanks to him that sat on the throne, who liveth for ever and ever, 10 The four and twenty elders fall down before him that sat on the throne, and worship him that liveth for ever and ever, and cast their crowns before the throne, saying, 11 Thou art worthy, O Lord, to receive glory and honour and power: for thou hast created all things, and for thy pleasure they are and were created*" (Revelation 4:8-11).

"*2 And I heard a voice from heaven, as the voice of many waters, and as the voice of a great thunder: and **I heard the voice of harpers harping with their harps: *3 And they sung as it were a new song before the throne**, and before the four beasts, and the elders: and no man could learn that song but the hundred and forty and four thousand, which were redeemed from the earth*" (Revelation 14:2-3).

Chapter Twenty-nine

Multitude of Angels

A ccording to Scripture, there are multitudes of angels around the throne of God. For example, we know there are twenty-four elders (Revelation 4:4) and four beasts (Revelation 4:6) around the throne of God. As this is the case, it can be deduced there are multitudes of angels round about the throne of God from Scripture.

"11 And I beheld, and I heard the voice of many angels round about the throne and the beasts and the elders: and the number of them was ten thousand times ten thousand, and thousands of thousands" (Revelation 5:11).

When you look closely at this scripture, it says "the beasts and the elders"; we know how many beasts and elders they are. So therefore, the figure Revelation 5:11 refers to is the number of angels "ten thousand times ten thousand and thousands of thousands".

That must be simply amazing!

Chapter Thirty

Rewards for Those Who Have Been Through Great Tribulation

T he Lord is a rewarder, and He rewards those who dili-
gently seek Him (Hebrews 11:6). He rewards us for our
works, which we have looked at in another chapter.

However, did you know there are rewards for those who have
gone through great tribulation?

"*13 And one of the elders answered, saying unto me, What are
these which are arrayed in white robes? and whence came
they? 14 And I said unto him, Sir, thou knowest. And he said to
me, **These are they which came out of great tribulation,
and have washed their robes, and made them white in***

the blood of the Lamb. [15] Therefore are they before the throne of God, and serve him day and night in his temple: and he that sitteth on the throne shall dwell among them. [16] They shall hunger no more, neither thirst any more; neither shall the sun light on them, nor any heat. [17] For the Lamb which is in the midst of the throne shall feed them, and shall lead them unto living fountains of waters: and God shall wipe away all tears from their eyes" (Revelation 7:13-17).

Let us look closely at the above scriptures; those who have come out of great tribulation are:

- Before the throne of God and serve Him day and night in His temple
- God shall dwell among them
- They shall hunger no more
- They shall thirst no more
- The sun shall not light on them nor any heat
- Jesus Christ shall feed them
- Jesus Christ shall lead them into living fountains of waters
- God shall wipe away all tears from their eyes

That is simply amazing!

Chapter Thirty-one

The Saints Will Reign on the Earth With Christ

According to Scripture, we will reign on this earth with Christ for one thousand years. During this time, the enemy will be bound for the duration of our reign on this earth with Jesus Christ.

"And I saw an angel come down from heaven, having the key of the bottomless pit and a great chain in his hand. ² And he laid hold on the dragon, that old serpent, which is the Devil, and Satan, and bound him a thousand years, ³ And cast him into the bottomless pit, and shut him up, and set a seal upon him, that he should deceive the nations no more, till the thousand years should be fulfilled: and after that he must be loosed a little season. ⁴ And I saw thrones, and they sat upon them, and judgment was given unto them: and I saw the souls of them that were beheaded for the witness of Jesus, and for the

word of God, and which had not worshipped the beast, neither his image, neither had received his mark upon their foreheads, or in their hands; **and they lived and reigned with Christ a thousand years**" (Revelation 20:1-4).

How are we sure this reign means here on earth? A few verses in this same chapter show us:

"*7 And when the thousand years are expired, Satan shall be loosed out of his prison, 8 And shall go out to deceive the nations which are in the four quarters of the earth, Gog, and Magog, to gather them together to battle: the number of whom is as the sand of the sea. 9* **And they went up on the breadth of the earth, and compassed the camp of the saints about, and the beloved city: and fire came down from God out of heaven, and devoured them**" (Revelation 20:7-9).

So, we can see that this camp was on earth.

Chapter Thirty-two

Clothing of the Saints

As a believer, did you know we have clothing? The Book of Revelation tells us that righteousness is our clothing.

"*7 Let us be glad and rejoice, and give honour to him: for the marriage of the Lamb is come, and his wife hath made herself ready. 8 And to her was granted that she should be arrayed in fine linen, clean and white: **for the fine linen is the righteousness of saints**"* (Revelation 19:7-8).

Therefore, we can see that righteousness is our clothing.

Chapter Thirty-three

Thanksgiving Is Taking Place

W e are told to thank God in all things (1 Thessalonians 5:18). But, did you know that thanksgiving is taking place in heaven?

*"And all the angels stood round about the throne, and about the elders and the four beasts, and fell before the throne on their faces, and worshipped God, 12 Saying, Amen: Blessing, and glory, and wisdom, **and thanksgiving**, and honour, and power, and might, be unto our God for ever and ever. Amen"* (Revelation 7:11-12).

*"16 And the four and twenty elders, which sat before God on their seats, fell upon their faces, and worshipped God, 17 Saying, **We give thee thanks, O Lord God Almighty, which art, and wast, and art to come; because thou hast taken***

to thee thy great power, and hast reigned" (Revelation 11:16-17).

Chapter Thirty-four

Loving the Lord Should Be Our First Priority

W hile this has been mentioned in a previous chapter, we will look into this warning in detail.

The Lord commended all the hard work of this church in Ephesus; however, they had left their first love.

"Unto the angel of the church of Ephesus write; These things saith he that holdeth the seven stars in his right hand, who walketh in the midst of the seven golden candlesticks; **2** *I know thy works, and thy labour, and thy patience, and how thou canst not bear them which are evil: and thou hast tried them which say they are apostles, and are not, and hast found them liars:* **3** *And hast borne, and hast patience, and for my name's sake hast laboured, and hast not fainted.* **4** ***Nevertheless I have somewhat against thee, because thou hast left thy***

first love. ⁵ Remember therefore from whence thou art
fallen, and repent, and do the first works; or else I will
come unto thee quickly, and will remove thy candlestick
out of his place, except thou repent" (Revelation 2:1-5).

To show how important this is to the Lord, He was ready to
remove the church if they did not repent. The candlesticks
are the churches according to Revelation 1:20.

This simply tells us that loving the Lord should be our first
priority; everything else should stem from our relationship
and fellowship with the Lord. Putting first things first is a
spiritual safety net.

Chapter Thirty-five

The Root of All Deception

T he enemy is the source and root of all deception. This is why as believers; we must know the truth and have good discernment.

*"And the great dragon was cast out, that old serpent, called the Devil, and Satan, **which deceiveth the whole world:** he was cast out into the earth, and his angels were cast out with him"* (Revelation 12:9).

Chapter Thirty-six

There Is No Respect of Persons With God!

D own here on earth, sometimes, we tend to classify people, and while we need to honour others, as far as Scripture is concerned, it applies to whosoever.

This is one reason we all need to stay humble.

"*And whosoever was not found written in the book of life was cast into the lake of fire*" (Revelation 20:15).

"*⁶ And he said unto me, It is done. I am Alpha and Omega, the beginning and the end. I will give unto him that is athirst of the fountain of the water of life freely*" (Revelation 21:6).

"*7 He that overcometh shall inherit all things; and I will be his God, and he shall be my son*" (Revelation 21:7).

Chapter Thirty-seven

The Power of the Blood of Jesus

J esus Christ our Lord has washed us from our sins in His own blood. Therefore, all we must do is receive the sacrifice that Jesus Christ has paid to redeem man back to God. This is simply by making Jesus Christ the Lord and Saviour of our lives (Romans 10:9-10; Acts 4:12).

"*5 And from Jesus Christ, who is the faithful witness, and the first begotten of the dead, and the prince of the kings of the earth. Unto him that loved us, **and washed us from our sins in his own blood**"* (Revelation 1:5).

"*9 And they sung a new song, saying, Thou art worthy to take the book, and to open the seals thereof: for thou wast slain, **and hast redeemed us to God by thy blood out of every** *kindred, and tongue, and people, and nation*" (Revelation 1:9).

Chapter Thirty-eight

What About the Rapture?

T here will definitely be a catching up ("rapture") of the saints, but nobody knows the day.

"*13 But I would not have you to be ignorant, brethren, concerning them which are asleep, that ye sorrow not, even as others which have no hope. 14 For if we believe that Jesus died and rose again, even so them also which sleep in Jesus will God bring with him. 15 For this we say unto you by the word of the Lord, that we which are alive and remain unto the coming of the Lord shall not prevent them which are asleep. 16 For the Lord himself shall descend from heaven with a shout, with the voice of the archangel, and with the trump of God: and the dead in Christ shall rise first: 17 **Then we which are alive and remain shall be caught up together with them in the clouds, to meet the Lord in the air: and so shall we ever be with the Lord***" **(1 Thessalonians 4:13-17).**

So, we can see from the above scriptures that there will be a rapture. Therefore, the priority of every believer is not to be caught unawares (Luke 21:34).

The Bible says no one knows the day or hour but God the Father only (Matthew 24:36).

In the Book of Revelation, it is not so clear when the rapture will take place; however, let us have a look at this scripture:

"*13 And I heard a voice from heaven saying unto me, Write, Blessed are the dead which die in the Lord from henceforth: Yea, saith the Spirit, that they may rest from their labours; and their works do follow them.* **14 And I looked, and behold a white cloud, and upon the cloud one sat like unto the Son of man, having on his head a golden crown, and in his hand a sharp sickle. 15 And another angel came out of the temple, crying with a loud voice to him that sat on the cloud, Thrust in thy sickle, and reap: for the time is come for thee to reap; for the harvest of the earth is ripe. 16 And he that sat on the cloud thrust in his sickle on the earth; and the earth was reaped**" (Revelation 14:13-16).

This is the closest scripture to the rapture occurring in the Book of Revelation. However, we know that in other scriptures, the Lord is coming back with the clouds (Matthew 26:64), and a sickle is used to reap something.

As for when this will happen, no man knows, but the wise virgins will ensure they are always ready.

Yes, there will be signs (2 Thessalonians 2:2-10) before the Lord's return, but no man knows the day nor hour, only God the Father does.

Chapter Thirty-nine

The Angelic Messages

There will be a point where angels will give messages. According to Revelation 14, the following will happen:

- An angel will preach the everlasting gospel (Revelation 14:6-7).
- An angel will declare what has happened to Babylon (Revelation 14:8).
- An angel warning people about worshipping the beast and receiving his mark (Revelation 14:9-12).

There would be no warnings if people could not respond to them. An angel preaching the everlasting gospel and an angel warning about the beast and his mark are expressions of the love of God. God loves people, and He does not want anyone to perish.

The wise give their hearts and lives to Jesus Christ now. There is so much treasure in Christ. The Bible describes this as "unsearchable riches", and everyone needs to receive the love of the truth (2 Thessalonians 2:10).

Chapter Forty

The Lord Has Armies

The Lord has an army in heaven.

"*12 His eyes were as a flame of fire, and on his head were many crowns; and he had a name written, that no man knew, but he himself. 13 And he was clothed with a vesture dipped in blood: and his name is called The Word of God. **14 And the armies which were in heaven followed him upon white horses, clothed in fine linen, white and clean**"* (Revelation 19:12-14).

Taking a look at this scripture, it is not revealed what the armies in heaven consist of. All we know is that these armies are upon white horses and clothed in fine linen, white and clean.

Could these be part of what Elisha's servant saw when Elisha asked the Lord to open the eyes of his servant?

"*15 And when the servant of the man of God was risen early, and gone forth, behold, an host compassed the city both with horses and chariots. And his servant said unto him, Alas, my master! how shall we do? 16 And he answered, Fear not: for they that be with us are more than they that be with them. 17 And Elisha prayed, and said, Lord, I pray thee, open his eyes, that he may see.* **And the Lord opened the eyes of the young man; and he saw: and, behold, the mountain was full of horses and chariots of fire round about Elisha**" (2 Kings 6:15-17).

Chapter Forty-one

Our Spirits Are Living Entities

According to Scripture, man has three parts: spirit, soul, and body (1 Thessalonians 5:23).

Our spirit is referred to as the "inner man" (2 Corinthians 4:16). Note the phrase "man".

Our spirits are living entities that will live forever in some place. For the believer in Christ, their destination is heaven.

"And the temple was filled with smoke from the glory of God, and from his power; ***and no man was able to enter into the temple,*** *till the seven plagues of the seven angels were fulfilled"* (Revelation 15:8).

Note the phrase "no man". We know flesh and blood do not inherit the Kingdom of God (1 Corinthians 15:50); therefore, the word "man" here is not referring to our flesh and blood.

The Bible says our corruptible body must wear incorruptible (1 Corinthians 15:53). In other words, there is life after this life, and we will remain as living entities.

Chapter Forty-two

Conclusion

We will do ourselves a lot of injustice if we reduce the Book of Revelation to the bowls of wrath. And yes, while the book tells us about the wrath to come, the believer in Christ has been delivered (1 Thessalonians 1:10).

There is so much beautiful and glorious content about the person of Jesus Christ, His passion for people, and the description of heaven that will ignite every believer and bring the sinner to the feet of Jesus.

In the warnings to the churches in many places, you will see the phrase, "He who has an ear to hear, let him hear". The wise will respond to God's love and the correction He brings across our way.

We must remember that the Lord will not tell us to do what we cannot do. God is love (1 John 4:8) and has sent His Son to pay the ultimate price.

"For God so loved the world, that he gave his only begotten Son, that whosoever believeth in him should not perish, but have everlasting life" (John 3:16).

The remedy for mankind is simple—receive Jesus Christ as Lord and Saviour. He loves people and loves you.

I hope this book has been a blessing to you!

Salvation Prayer

F ather God, I come to you in Jesus' name. I admit that I am a sinner, and I now receive the sacrifice that Jesus Christ paid for me.

I confess with my mouth the Lord Jesus, and I believe in my heart that God raised Him from the dead.

I now declare that Jesus Christ is my Lord and Saviour.

Thank you, Father, for saving me in Jesus' name.

I am now your child. Amen.

If you've said this prayer for the first time, send an email to bisiwriter@outlook.com.
Start reading your Bible and ask the Lord to guide you to a good church.

About The Author

Bisi Oladipupo has been a Christian for many years and lives in the United Kingdom with her family.

Bisi attended a few Bible colleges, and she has completed a diploma in Biblical Studies from a UK Bible college.

She is a teacher of God's Word, coordinates Bible studies, and has a YouTube channel at https://www.youtube.com/c/BisiO ladipupo123.

She writes regularly, and her website is www.inspired-words.org

Her author page is www.bisiwriter.com

You can contact Bisi by email at bisiwriter@outlook.com.

Also By Bisi

The Twelve Apostles of Jesus Christ: Lessons We Can Learn

The Lord's Cup in Communion: The Significance of taking the Lord's Supper

Different Ways to Receive Healing from Scripture and Walk in Health

Believing on The Name of Jesus Christ: What Every Believer Needs to Know

The Mind and your Christian Walk: The Impact of the mind on our Christian walk

Relationship Skills in the Bible: Scriptural Principles of relating to others

The Nature of God's Kingdom: The Characteristics of the Kingdom of God

The Person of the Holy Spirit

Lightning Source UK Ltd.
Milton Keynes UK
UKHW010736270722
406409UK00002B/343